The Great Scissor Hunt

The Great Scissor Hunt

Jessica K. Hylton

HEADMISTRESS PRESS

Copyright © 2016 by Jessica K. Hylton
All rights reserved.

ISBN-13: 978-0-9979149-6-2
ISBN-10: 0997914963

This book may not be reproduced, in whole or in part, including illustrations, in any form (beyond that permitted by Sections 107 and 108 of the U.S. Copyright Law and except by reviewers for the public press), without written permission from the publishers.

Cover art © 2013 Hannah Barrett. *Help Desk,* 76" x 42"
Cover & book design by Mary Meriam.

PUBLISHER
Headmistress Press
60 Shipview Lane
Sequim, WA 98382
Telephone: 917-428-8312
Email: headmistresspress@gmail.com
Website: headmistresspress.blogspot.com

For
The string of bad decisions I'll never regret

Contents

Satsumas	1
Birdbrained Emotions	2
Headlines	4
Elephants, fingers, and loneliness.	6
Holding a Baby	8
The Stare of Plastic Owls	9
Encounter	11
Closeted	12
Pieces of Me	14
Hobbled	15
Eros, Psyche, and Plumbers.	17
Pickup Lines	18
Rocking	19
Fly Away	20
Second Chances	21
Academic Pole Dance	22
The One That Got Away	23
There comes a point in any relationship	24
First Time	26
Chameleon	27
Holiday Cheer	28
About the Author	31
Acknowledgments	33

Satsumas

I blinked the road back into place
As I turned my Mustang
Toward a tired destination
Another night with too much
Alcohol and not enough sleep
But at least I'm young
Enough it hasn't caught me
Yet

On the roadside sat
A man advertising fresh fruit
Satsumas—said the sign
Featuring letters that should
Have been drawn by a child
Old age doesn't prevent criticism
It just leaves a guilty after taste

Of course he'd be selling
Satsumas—Satsumas
What a vicious fruit
Nothing more than a stunted orange

But there's something
Intoxicating about the taste of skin
Designed to peel away

Never knowing if the moment
Will be sweet
Or if it had been plucked
Too soon

Birdbrained Emotions

They say to get over someone
You're supposed to pick up a new hobby
And apparently the most cathartic
Are the hobbies where you make something
So you bring a woodworking bench
Past the film cameras, the roller skates, the bass guitar
And hope that a new birdhouse
Will take away memories
Better than the temporary
Reprieve granted by neon flavored shots
And long legs that walk in directions
You don't really want to go

But one birdhouse only leads to another
A gateway carpentry
And pretty soon the whole living room
Is filled with 353 birdhouses
Then you realize you don't even like birds
Fucking feathered freaks that shit on their own food
Why do they deserve to live in such palaces
While you can barely afford a one bedroom apartment
That smells of burnt out cigarettes and stale new beginnings

In fact you hate birds
You think about taking all the houses
Outside and lighting them on fire
To be rid of the clutter
But while you're looking for matches
You run across a keepsake that you shouldn't still keep
And pretty soon you're staring at a blank text message
Trying to think of the right thing to say to the wrong person

Thinking honesty is the best option
You start typing out "I mis—"
But you can't even stand to look at the words
As if somehow seeing them makes
Them more real and you know honesty
Is only appreciated by hearts that want to beat
Not by those looking for refuge behind walls

You throw the phone across
The birdhouse mountain range
And do the only thing you know
How to do at this point
Start on number 354

Headlines

You woke up bitching like always
You were thirsty, the sun was too bright
I was nothing more than a mistake
In the days, weeks, months
Christ... Years We'd been fucking
You never changed
The late night I need yous that turned
Into the usual good morning goodbyes

I steered the car onto the road
And reminded myself that last night
Was the real last night
As you yammered about the bridge
Being out up ahead
I didn't alter my course
And you didn't shut up

"This is it. We are going to die
Together and the headlines will read
The two Crazies finally got
What they deserved."
You kept on and I never took
My eyes off the road

We made it almost to the blockade
Before I pushed in the clutch
Cut the wheel and slid down
A back alley you didn't know existed
You seemed pleased we hadn't died
And I took the moment of silence
To tell you I needed to piss

I parked at a gas station
Walked past the bathroom
Grabbed your favorite Gatorade
A couple packets of Advil
And a pair of aviators

The salesclerk made me pay before
He let me bend the nose pieces back
So you wouldn't get self- conscious
About the size of your nose

When I got back to the car
I tossed the bag in your direction
Without looking you put them on
And were surprised they fit your face
I stayed quiet

You didn't say thank you
You just let your hand crawl
Over to my knee where it belonged
And I knew if I wanted it to stay
I had to appear uninterested

That's when I realized
You were right
"This is it.
We are going to die together
And the headlines will read the two Crazies
Finally got what they deserved."

Elephants, fingers, and loneliness.

The elephant has arthritis
Or at least that's what the sign
Told us after we'd followed
One of my attempts to fix
How she broke your heart
By giving you all of mine
I don't even remember
What she had done or what
She hadn't done that time
But it was big enough
I knew it could only be conquered
By seeing an elephant
And despite the tropical heat
And growing obesity rate in America
I knew we would be headed
On quite the quest to find one

About an hour into our drive
You ran your fingers between
Mine and flipped over my hand
Only to trace the fermata on my wrist
And ask what it meant
When I explained you exclaimed
"So you're asking for someone to hold your hand?"
Before I could respond
You turned over our hands again
And revealed your own wrist
Which read "I am."
My favorite author's words
You misquoted because you
Got the line from Google
Instead of the book it didn't matter
To me it affirmed our intentions
Love not written in the skies
But scarred into wrists
Of two razor blade wielding confessionalists

As we got closer to the elephant
The distance between us kept
Becoming more and more majestic
I smiled for pictures we never took
And ordered a snow cone flavored blue
Because it was the taste
We'd both gotten used to

By the time we got to the sign
I knew we were just like that damn elephant
Big, wonderful, and rare
But we weren't going anywhere
Because you couldn't believe
In the honesty careless lovers
Make us outgrow years before we should
And it was all I had left to offer

Holding a Baby

I was tricked into the only
Time I have ever held a baby
A friend of a friend shouted
Here and took off sprinting
I was expecting to grab on
To a beer or maybe an American Spirit
Not a poop producing machine
That passed itself off
As a miniature human

I tried to hold the thing
At arm's length, but I hadn't
Been to the gym like I resolved to
And after about 30 seconds
My elbows started quivering
Trying to get a grip
On the morbidly obese creature
So I had to bring it to my lap
But it kept staring at me plotting
When it was going to vomit
All over my mostly clean shirt

It had already sucked the life
From one woman—infecting
Her with its parasitic motivations
So I sat it down on the ground
And tried to escape
But it kept falling over unable
To support its own bulk
And attracting unwanted attention
With its incessant wails

I cautiously extended one toe
Placed it firmly on the slobbering
Beast's back and made
Sure it stayed upright
I guess even I have some
Maternal instinct

The Stare of Plastic Owls

I was sitting in the audience
Of a play I was technically
A part of when I took notice
Of a plastic owl glaring down
From atop a decrepit safe
That decomposed publicly
At the same rate as Wild West
Outlaws decayed in closed coffins

The owl sat silent its eyes
Boring in my direction drilling
Pumping up my memory
Of the glass owl
I left on your windshield
And the "owl always love you"
Note scribbled in childlike letters
Tucked in tightly underneath
The wiper blades

I fidgeted in my costume and reminded
Myself I was supposed to blend
Into the crowd as I fantasized
About taking a baseball bat
To that smug owl
I knew it would smash apart
Maybe it would take a bit more force
Than we did
But promises are always hollow
Regardless of the certainty
Of their paint jobs
And finely brushed details

How much more lifelike
Destruction makes us all
The owl's shards feathering the ground
Perhaps even moving in the wind
But I knew nothing could ruin

Its terrible eyes
They were the kind of eyes
That never close but never see
They were your eyes

I dropped my own to the floor
The music cued me to move
And I danced away
Knowing emptiness watched
My every move

Encounter

I found you in a
Bathroom filled with
Broken taps
And fragmented mirrors
After following the advice
Of a prolific number
I got off a wall

Splintered glass
Lied as it showed
My body fully
Clothed. For my shirt
Could not bear
The ravishment of
Your eyes

In an instant
You dragged a match
Across harsh terrain
Causing its head to
Erupt in fiery wetness
That spattered across
My skin

My thighs trembled
Seeking movement
My feet denied as
My brain and heart
Battled viciously
Among the smell
Of sweat and urine

Your parting smile
Proved my struggle
Futile—Needless
Casualties crowded to
See your spent match
Floating inside my
Flaccid reflection

Closeted

An academic excuse
For a friend disturbed
My contrived persona
By loudly proclaiming
He wanted to introduce
Me to someone I would
Love

I turned expecting to
Meet yet another suit
In dire need of a
Personality never
Guessing that suit
Would be you

Your new lover sterilized
Your eyes with the dullness
Of his passion and erased
The laugh lines we
Drew together as we
Tried to sketch out an existence

Introductions were short
As we both feigned
Complete ignorance but
Knowing fully how to
Make the other climax
With the slightest stroke

Memories I had tried to burn
Resurrected themselves
In the ash of your face
I fought to stay in control
This me did not know—
Could not know you

You quickly dismissed
Yourself to the restroom
Reminding me of an old hunger
And the times I'd slam
You against the bathroom
Stall feeling your thighs

Demand the touch of my hips
And tasting lingering remnants
Of your last Marlboro 72 never
Thinking your lips could so
Easily forget the flavor of mine
I closed my eyes picturing

Liberating your breasts from
The confines of your socially
Accepted lifestyle—but what
Good's a revolution when the
People are still loyal to the
Previous dictator?

Go ahead with your
Mattel® encouraged relationship
His inappropriate genitalia
Will eventually make
You forget your own

Pieces of Me

I watched her slide
My thighs into her jeans
She winced as she dissected
The purpling bruise
Spreading across our hips

I'd worked hard for that mark
Pain's agoraphobic
It remains invisible
Even when trauma demands
It take center stage

She was going out again
With another boy
Whose name I either forgot
Or I didn't want to remember

I felt her lick my teeth
Before she chastised my recklessness
Mid-date she'd reduce me
To a proclivity to clumsiness
And smile away my snarl

I let her prance out
With my feet in her heels
She'll be back
She always comes back

And I will wrap my arms
Around her knees
As we slip into sleep

Hobbled

"Come with me"
Your hands tremble
As you started peeling
The label off your
Tasteless low calorie
Michelob—I hate this new
Change. Him calling you fat
In hopes of starving
The gayness out of you
Like some sort of
Disease

You start sputtering reasons
To stay—I have to be careful
Too much pressure and I'll
Flood your engines, but not
Enough and we'll never go
Anywhere "I don't mean
Not come back, but come
Down with me for a bit
You, me, and the open road"
Your eyes search mine
For what I can't tell
Freedom maybe?

Like when you were in
High school and you'd
Ride around with your
Friends smoking someone
Else's Luckies and knowing
That somehow you were
Going to make the world
Pay attention. I was on the
Same streets alone in
My convertible out running
The cops as I drove intoxicated
By the night

No we can't go back to
The unbridled ignorance
Of our teenage years but
We don't have to languish
Here as we play house and
Pretend we're not turning
Into our parents. Take my
Hand and let's go. Never
In search of a destination
Always in search of a
Breath that isn't polluted
With other people's ideals

I pushed, and you didn't
Ignite in an explosion of
Pure happiness as my foolish
Heart had hoped but maybe
I sparked a slow burn
That with each drag
Brings you closer to understanding
But for now, I'll pack my
Bags and load the car
Wondering if you'll be in
The passenger's seat when
I turn the key

Eros, Psyche, and Plumbers.

Plumbing lines never get me horny
But yet that's what the poor sap
Trying to pick me up prattled
About for at least half an hour
Before you came in with your hips
Directing the tempo of the music
Pouring out of the jukebox

I thought fast—hoping to figure out
A strategy to get away from the guy
Trying to snake my uterus
When you clogged his advances
Sliding your thighs on top of mine
Once you had flushed a chair out for yourself
You climbed off my lap
Neither one of us willing to so openly test
Aphrodite's patience.

Pickup Lines

Attractive people are never interested in me
They take one look at the elbow
I split open because I can't figure out
How to balance while walking
Or at my right eye which stays pointed
To the left because I've said,
"Hey watch this" one too many times

So when I saw the unusually clean hipster
Undercutting the careless placement of her feet
With a surgically straight back
Sucking on a smoke with the grace
Of Clint Eastwood
I couldn't resist striking out swinging
Wildly wanting only to piss off the air

"You'd be a lot better looking without that cigarette"
I asked for both the smoke and her number

She left me smiling
With neither

Rocking

"I need your help with my poetry"
That's how she got me there
Where I knew her partner
Slept on the other side
Of the wall I leaned against

She scuttled around trying
To be the good hostess
"Do you want another beer?"
No.
"Do you need a hat to keep you warm?"
No.
"Are we just friends?"

I asked about the rocking chair
On its side its bones unable
To even bear the weight of a child
She looked at me with sorrow
"Termites. I watched them destroy
It and all it did was rock
Back and forth."

I should have known then
Maybe I did know then
But I didn't want to know then

So when she came back out
With her poems written in
Tight clean letters and asked
"What should I change?"
I couldn't think of a thing

Fly Away

Airports always stink of goodbyes
I know you're not her
But when her words tumble
From your lips
What I know becomes
As blurred as an 18 year old's
Grasp on philosophy
What is really real?

'I'm coming back'
You mouth from the other
Side of the safety glass
That separates lover from lover
Children from parents
And terrorists from planes

It's funny how a few people
Who forgot how to care
Breed entire generations
Of people who never get the chance
To learn because contact ceases
To caress and becomes contamination

Second Chances

I wasn't even in the bar
Just stumbling near one
When a blue eyed bad decision
Led to about five more

Before I knew it
I was in her bed telling the story
Of when I was young
I never wanted anyone
To go down on me
Because that's where
The pee came out

And how ironic it was
That I eventually figured out
I was a lesbian
When she put her thigh
On my shoulder
And asked if we were do
This or not

I guess I was drunker
Than I thought I was
Cause the next thing
I knew I was at your door
Saying all the things

I should have said six months ago
To ears that had lost
All desire to hear
And wondering if we
Were going to do this
Or not

Academic Pole Dance

After spending the weekend
With my girlfriend's parents
Who aren't okay with the fact
My girlfriend has a girlfriend

I stopped into a strip club
To see how men's desire
For pussy was more respectable
Than my intended illegal marriage

All of the expected cast
Shadowed stereotypes
The wimpy men growing hard
With the unattainable at hand

The judgmental women
Looking down on the ballerinas
While secretly hungering
For an ass that tight

The crowd moaned
The anticipated excitement
While exposing more of its self
Than the dancing girls

I looked down to see academia
Barely covering my own privates
Nothing more than a sheepskin G-string
But at least it didn't chafe

The One That Got Away

A student asked me, "what kind
Of poet are you? Can you slickly
Slide thick consonants
To new meanings?"

I told her I wasn't one for sounds
As I preferred to leave that mastery
To the melodic jackhammers chiseling
Away at the median while I drive
Past staring at a street sign
Warning Butte LaRose next exit

Butte LaRose becomes LaRosa
And I'm back on the second barstool
From the end surrounded by college kids
Removed from current students
In age but never in intentions
Back before Finnegan needed a wake
And we still thought we could write stories
Instead of simply falling into predictable plot lines
Carrying the groceries and twenty new pounds
That keep our reckless fantasies
Buried as we wait for Alzheimer's salvation

Halfway through my reasoning
She let her pencil take a vacation
Though she did politely let me finish
Before concluding, "So, you're not
A very good poet."

I laughed and said, "I guess not"

There comes a point in any relationship

When the all day sex-o-thons slack off
And things start taking on deeper meanings
Kind of like that poem in your high school
English class when your teacher advocated
A flea was some kind of symbol for sex
And all you got out of it was
Who would fuck a flea
A byproduct of decomposition

So this morning when she asked me
To pick up a stamp I knew
We weren't really talking about a stamp
But rather some sort of metaphor
For the stagnation of our existence
I could have just gone to the post office
But paying a balding man with a weirdly short tie
49¢ seemed about as heroic as slaying a windmill

I didn't need an ordinary stamp
I needed the stamp of all stamps
An epic quest to prove my love
Hadn't gone stale like the uneaten bananas
We continually buy with the best intentions
And forget about until either the smell
Or the cloud of fruit flies reminds us of our failure
I needed a challenge
I wanted to suffer
To earn that stamp

So I asked a friend
Who stole one from a gigantic roll
Peeling one off—leaving
The sticky side exposed
And my fate dependent
On the quality of USPS merchandise

When she said the lawn mower wasn't working
And looked at me like I should know how to fix it
I knew I was in trouble
The only thing I knew about mowers
Came from the three years I spent working on a golf course
Where a man named Perry would fix them
After I took my steel steeds through a fence on hole 7

He was a good guy
The kind that nicknamed me Sunshine
But also invited me to the Blue Jay Motel
For a one night stand he knew would kill him
I never introduced him to my mother

I changed the spark plug
The oil, the fuel line, the air filter
And my perspective on longevity
But the mower wouldn't run

She even joined me
Googling answers to the unknowable
As I covered myself in gasoline and bourbon
A heartbroken Tibetan monk
Amid Chinese construction
And the proof that even "made in America"
Doesn't last forever

First Time

I feel my weakness
Weeping down my thighs
At the unrestrained
Lust of your mouth

The implicit touch
Softly nuzzling
Women weep
Woman weak

Stay your passion-filled caress
I can smell your fears
Laced with mine

Chameleon

She pranced into the bar each shod heel thunking across
The wooden floor drenched in spilled courage and suppressed sadness
Arching her neck elegantly, she allowed her would be jockeys to inspect
Her quality—fine hindquarters, a little thick around the girth
Turn her around one more time

The Bud drinker on the last stool was the first to try his hand
In an instant she pounced—purring each promise and growling
Toward his groin. Finding a less than worthy prize underneath
Her paw, she tossed the young scrap to the less selective members
Of her pride

Next the white wine sipping seasoned veteran
Presented her with an orange intoxication which she
Nibbled on nervously her ears lengthening at the drone of his voice
"Watch me pull an erection out of my pants" Never one for magic
She made him disappear

One by one they approached, one by one they failed
Seeing only what she wanted them to see

Holiday Cheer

She was fiddling with the radio as we waited
For the warm air to chase our breath away
When she asked why do people
Get so depressed about holidays?

The question was so simple
That of course it had no answer
I would have preferred a theoretical
Debate about the legitimacy of postmodernism

"Because people remember all they have lost"
Was the first response I could think of
But I knew it was a lie before I closed my lips
You don't remember what you've lost

But what you could have lost
You keep the setting, the characters
And change the plot to match
The holiday you wish you'd had

That drunk uncle you avoided
Because he'd give you a .25 cent
Pack of gum as payment
For pinching your ass

Becomes a jolly merrymaker
Who made your grandmother's day
The same grandmother who demanded
You cut up potatoes and barked

At you to not bleed on the food when the knife
Satisfied its own hunger with the flesh
Of your thumb becomes a tough old bird
That you admire for her tenacity

But in reality, your uncle
Still is a pervert
And your grandmother
Is still a bitch

I resolved then and there to forget
The ghosts of holidays past
And try to form something new
With the innocence beside me

Finding cheer in actual human contact
Rather than the single
12 oz servings I needed
Three of before I felt anything

But the holidays fought back
And I found myself surrounded
By good people and delightful foods
Unable to connect to the moment

And knowing that next year
I would lament the moment's perfection
And I realized
Maybe I hadn't lied at all

About the Author

Jessica K. Hylton is currently a Visiting Assistant Professor of English at Lock Haven University. She holds a PhD in Creative Writing from the University of Louisiana at Lafayette and writes most of her poems on her cellphone while driving. She has wrecked three cars, but she finished her dissertation. Hylton's collection *Scatter; Or, James Joyce Always Makes Me Think of Boobs* is forthcoming from Knut House Press, and her individual poems have been featured in *Lavender Review, Cliterature, Visceral Uterus,* and many others. She is the founding editor of *Fermata Publishing,* and the layout editor of *Bateau Ivre.*

Acknowledgments

My thanks to the editors of the following publications, in which these poems first appeared:

Cliterature: "Second Chances"

East Coast Literary Review: "Birdbrained Emotions"

Lavender Review: "Eros, Psyche, and Plumbers."

Rat's Ass Review: "Headlines"

[Untitled] Publications: "Satsumas," "The One That Got Away"

Visceral Uterus: "Holding a Baby"

Headmistress Press Books

Lovely - Lesléa Newman
Teeth & Teeth - Robin Reagler
How Distant the City - Freesia McKee
Shopgirls - Marissa Higgins
Riddle - Diane Fortney
When She Woke She Was an Open Field - Hilary Brown
God With Us - Amy Lauren
A Crown of Violets - Renée Vivien tr. Samantha Pious
Fireworks in the Graveyard - Joy Ladin
Social Dance - Carolyn Boll
The Force of Gratitude - Janice Gould
Spine - Sarah Caulfield
Diatribe from the Library - Farrell Greenwald Brenner
Blind Girl Grunt - Constance Merritt
Acid and Tender - Jen Rouse
Beautiful Machinery - Wendy DeGroat
Odd Mercy - Gail Thomas
The Great Scissor Hunt - Jessica K. Hylton
A Bracelet of Honeybees - Lynn Strongin
Whirlwind @ Lesbos - Risa Denenberg
The Body's Alphabet - Ann Tweedy
First name Barbie last name Doll - Maureen Bocka
Heaven to Me - Abe Louise Young
Sticky - Carter Steinmann
Tiger Laughs When You Push - Ruth Lehrer
Night Ringing - Laura Foley
Paper Cranes - Dinah Dietrich
On Loving a Saudi Girl - Carina Yun
The Burn Poems - Lynn Strongin
I Carry My Mother - Lesléa Newman
Distant Music - Joan Annsfire
The Awful Suicidal Swans - Flower Conroy
Joy Street - Laura Foley
Chiaroscuro Kisses - G.L. Morrison
The Lillian Trilogy - Mary Meriam
Lady of the Moon - Amy Lowell, Lillian Faderman, Mary Meriam
Irresistible Sonnets - ed. Mary Meriam
Lavender Review - ed. Mary Meriam

www.ingramcontent.com/pod-product-compliance
Lightning Source LLC
Chambersburg PA
CBHW070042070426
42449CB00012BA/3145